ZOOM IN ON

THE MIDDLE AGES

ADAPTED BY
HAZEL MARY MARTELL

KINGFISHER

Contents

A Story

Information

An Activity

Information

An Activity

Information

Anecdotes

Information

A Test

A Game

Information

Stickers

Postcards

William's Return

The return of the son

"*D*ame Yolande," cried Doda, "I can see dust rising on the road. A horseman is coming! No, two horsemen!"

"Good heavens, do you think it is him already?"

"I think so," replied the servant. "The messenger told us two days, but your son must have been in such a hurry to return that a single day was enough."

"Good heavens," Dame Yolande said again. "My son! It is ten years since I have seen him, ten years since he left for the Crusades, ten years that he has been a prisoner of the Turks!" She turned to the guards. "Quickly, lower the drawbridge!"

A Story

There was a loud noise of hooves, then two horses came into the castle courtyard. William jumped to the ground and ran up to Dame Yolande.

"Mother, how good it is to see you again!"

"At last, it is you, my son!" Dame Yolande cried as she embraced him. "I hardly recognized you!"

"You shouldn't be so surprised," said William. "I was only fifteen when I left. But you, mother, haven't changed at all. And here is Master Albaldus. What good fortune! Do you remember how cross I made you when I refused to learn how to shoot a bow?"

"The only arms that you liked," Albaldus replied, "were – "

"– the sword," finished William. "I fear I was a difficult pupil. And here is Doda, my dear nurse! I hope you have forgiven all the naughty tricks I played on you!"

"I have forgotten them all," said Doda, laughing, "because I am so happy you have returned."

"Have you even forgotten the day when I tore up all the tablecloths to make ropes?"

Doda laughed again.

"Go and clean yourself up a little at the fountain, my son," suggested Dame Yolande, "while I give orders to prepare a feast. We must celebrate your return!"

William went towards the fountain, followed by his servant. "It's working," the man chuckled. "They think you are William. It's true that with your beard, you do resemble him."

"It's because it is such a long time since these people have seen him. Between fifteen and twenty-five years old, a person changes a lot."

"All the same, take care. I have the impression that they are suspicious, and that the old man was testing you when he spoke of the only arms that you liked."

"It is not too difficult. William and I were prisoners together for ten years, and we had plenty of time to talk. He described them so well that I recognized them all: the fat nurse with freckles, the mother, the old lame master of arms."

"What are we going to do now?"

"Don't worry about a thing. William can't do us any harm where he is. What we must do is take charge of the castle affairs. When everything is under our control, we will get rid of the mother and we will be rich. Rich!" He pushed up his sleeves and held his hands under the fountain's clear water.

Curious...

Dame Yolande was thoughtful. Her son had suffered for ten years in filthy prisons, and no doubt that was why he had changed so much. It must certainly be him, because he knew them all and remembered everything from his earlier life. When they were sitting down to dinner she said amiably: "Well, my son, you seem to like this cod pie."

"Yes indeed, it is delicious."

"Yet you used to hate it so!"

William looked squarely at Dame Yolande and burst out laughing. "That is because I have had a taste of prison and I have become less spoilt. When my stomach was tortured with hunger, I would have given my right hand for a slice of this pie."

Everyone started to laugh, and Dame Yolande was reassured: yes, this man was undoubtedly her son.

Then William said: "Rest assured, mother, I have avenged my father's assassination by the Turks by killing dozens of them with my own hands."

Dame Yolande shook her head without replying, then she left the dining hall followed by her servant.

"Doda, what do you say to that?"

"I don't know, Dame Yolande. It is true that after the death of your husband, we decided never to admit that he was burned to death for sorcery. We told everyone that he was killed by the Turks."

"But my son knew that was not true."

"After all this time, perhaps your son persuaded himself that his father was really a hero."

"Do you think so? He had no need to speak of it and open up old wounds. That surprises me."

Dame Yolande looked out of the window and remained thoughtful.

He who thought he was deceiving, was himself being deceived

The next day Dame Yolande called William to her chamber and announced: "My son, I have a surprise for you. Millicent, your foster-sister, has hurried over as soon as she heard of your return. Here she is."

William hesitated for a moment. A foster-sister? He couldn't remember the real William talking about a foster-sister! Already, he had noticed Dame Yolande react with the slightest movement of her head when he recalled the death of his father. Had William not told him the whole truth? He must not make any more mistakes.

"Millicent!" he cried happily. "I would not have recognized you! What a beautiful woman you have become!"

"Come now, was I not just as pretty when we were children?" retorted Millicent, laughing.

"Of course, you have always been pretty," William replied, "but I was too young to appreciate it."

Dame Yolande went away without saying

anything and retired to her room. William never had a foster-sister. She had invented Millicent herself and asked one of the servants to play the role. She had trapped him: this man was not William! Good grief! It was lucky for him that there were no dungeons in this castle! All the same, she had an idea. She called Doda.

The trap

Doda approached William's servant as he came out of the stables and looked to right and left before whispering: "Hey, you! I'd better warn you, as one servant to another, everything has been discovered! Tonight, your master will be captured by the guards. He is to be beheaded at dawn, and you with him."

The servant turned white.

"If I were you," said Doda, "I would flee, and quickly!"

"Flee? How?"

"First, tell me how you got to know William, and what has happened to him. Only then will I tell you how to escape."

"William? Well, William was freed from the Turkish jail at the same time as us. All three of us came back, but he..."

"What?"

"He was returning to a family – a castle – whereas we had nothing. Therefore, as my brother resembles him a little, we decided to pretend he was William."

"This man is your brother? Oh, what does it matter! What have you done with William? Tell me or my Lady will have both of you beheaded!"

"We threw him into the dungeons of a ruined castle."

"You devils! And I expect you left him without water or food so that he would die quickly and you would not have to worry about him returning! Which castle?"

"Tell me first how to escape."

"At the northwest tower there is a door that opens onto a staircase to the vaults. And where is the castle?"

"Two leagues from here, towards the south."

Rascals away!

It was the black of night. At the window of the keep, Dame Yolande and Doda listened. Suddenly, there was a great splash, then another – two descents into the water.

"That's good," said Doda. "They have opened the door that I pretended was the staircase to the vaults and fallen into the moat. In a few moments, they will climb out, frightened by their fall and numb with cold, and they will dash away as fast as they can."

"I hope the devil punishes them!" said Dame Yolande. "Alas! The hardest thing for me to bear is my unfulfilled desire to see my son again."

"Your son is not far away, Madam. I have sent some servants to collect him. Listen! See the torches over there? Are they not horses approaching?"

"I hear them," whispered Dame Yolande. "There are three. And my son is riding one of them."

"You are sure?"

"Certain," said Dame Yolande. "I feel it in my heart."

Medieval Life and

The Middle Ages lasted for 1,000 years from AD 500 to 1500. During this time, there were more than 15,000 castles in Europe and the Near East. Another name for this period in history is medieval times.

The castle dominated everything in the landscape.

The medieval landscape

Although there were towns and cities in medieval times, most people lived in small villages in the country. As well as the houses of the peasants and labourers, each village had a church and a manor house or castle where the local landowner lived. Usually there was also a windmill or water mill for grinding corn into flour to make bread.

The Church had an enormous influence on the lives of the people.

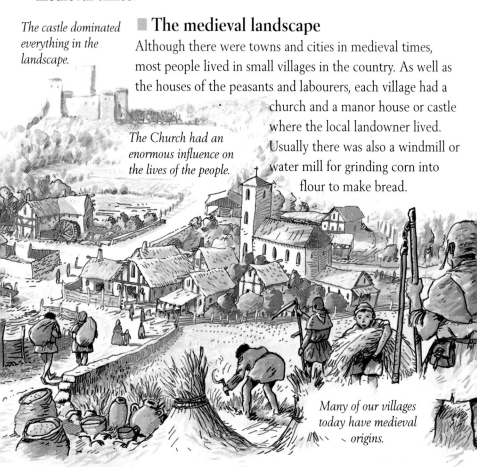

Many of our villages today have medieval origins.

Landscape

A hard life

Life was much harder in medieval times than it is today. People worked long hours. Houses were often cold and draughty, even for the rich. Running water was a rare luxury, and indoor lavatories were unknown until around 1200. If the harvest failed, people went hungry. They were then more likely to become ill and die.

A shorter lifespan

The average lifespan in medieval times was much less than it is today. This was because so many children died shortly after birth or in early infancy. Those who lived to be adults could die suddenly from diseases that are easily cured today. This meant the population remained small.

Staying put

Very few peasants ever ventured more than a few kilometres beyond the village they were born in. This was partly because they grew all the food they needed and made all their own clothes and tools, but also because travelling was difficult. Roads were just rough tracks, dusty in summer and muddy in winter.

Slow progress

Time was measured by the passing of the seasons. Sowing and harvest were repeated year after year. Life for one generation was much the same as for the one before and the one after. Progress came very slowly.

Life for the Peasants

In medieval Europe, nine out of ten people were peasants.

■ Houses

Peasants' houses had just one room, with a fire for heating and cooking. There were no chimneys, so smoke went out through the thatched roof. The floor was made from beaten earth and the walls were made from wattle and daub – branches woven together and plastered with mud. The small windows had no glass, but could be closed with wooden shutters.

■ Farming methods

Most villages had three large fields, each divided into several long strips. The strips were then divided amongst the villagers. They dug the soil with wooden spades and scattered the seed by hand, planting barley, oats, wheat or rye. In the 12th century, the horse collar was introduced. This allowed horses to pull the new, heavier ploughs, which had iron blades.

Peasants sold their surplus food to the city-dwellers who had no land of their own.

Information

■ The farming year

Each season brought its own tasks. In autumn, the peasants ploughed their strips of land and sowed seed for the spring in one field. In winter, they killed pigs for meat and repaired tools. In spring, they sowed more seed in the second field, leaving the third field lying *fallow*. In summer, they harvested their grain, keeping one third for next year's seed.

Fallow means left unploughed and unplanted for a year, to try and keep the land fertile.

■ Rent and service

The land the peasants worked on belonged to the lord of the manor. As payment for being allowed to grow their crops on it, they had to give him part of their produce and work on his land when he wanted them to. They also had to fight with him in times of war.

The peasants also had to pay the lord of the manor to grind their grain in his mill and bake bread in his oven.

The Castle

The castles were the homes and strongholds of powerful lords. They also sheltered the peasants in times of danger.

■ Building castles

The first castles were wooden fortresses built on top of an artificial mound called a motte. This gave a good view of the surrounding countryside. At the base were various outbuildings, in a fenced courtyard called a bailey. In the 12th century the wooden fortresses were replaced by strong stone keeps, and the baileys were surrounded by one or two thick stone walls with towers and a gatehouse.

■ Norman castles

In 1066, William of Normandy defeated King Harold at the Battle of Hastings and declared himself king of England. To stop people rebelling against him, he had castles built in all the major towns and let his supporters live in them.

■ Castle life

Each castle had its own lord, who lived in the keep with his family. His income came from the vast estates that surrounded his castle, so he could spend his time *hunting* in the forests and practising the arts of warfare. The lord entertained friends at great feasts, where they enjoyed watching jugglers and listening to minstrels, or troubadours, singing about knights and their adventures.

The lord hunted on horseback, using birds of prey or a bow and arrow. He also used dogs to collect his catch for him.

■ A siege

Castles were frequently surrounded and cut off by enemy troops. Then the drawbridge was raised and archers took up their positions on the walls. Boiling lead, oil and water were poured through holes, or machicolations, in the parapets at the top of the castle. The enemy attacked the outer wall with battering rams and threw flaming torches, but usually only gained access when the castle ran out of food and water.

Religion in Everyday

Christianity was the main religion in Europe in the Middle Ages. Everyone looked to the pope in Rome as the head of the Church. Beneath him in order of importance were the cardinals, the bishops and finally the priests.

■ The village church

Nearly every village had its own church where the local population went to Mass on Sunday. The priest was usually the only person in the village who could read and write. As well as performing religious duties, a good priest often treated the sick and helped the poor in the village.

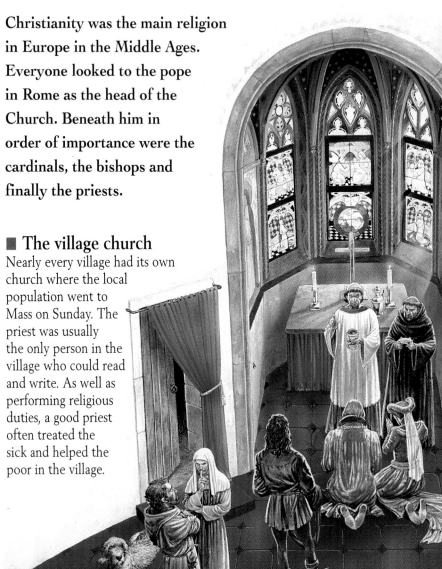

ife

Everyday rites

Religion played a part in everyone's life from the cradle to the grave. When a child was born, it was taken to church to be baptized. When a person was dying, the priest was brought to the house to give him or her the last sacraments or communion. The priest also married people, though he could not be married himself. He listened to their confessions and tried to make sure that everyone obeyed the Church's laws.

A life apart

The number of monasteries and nunneries increased in the Middle Ages, as many people shut themselves away from the world and dedicated their lives to religion. All monks and nuns spent a lot of time at prayer. They also worked hard, growing their own food as well as looking after travellers, the poor and the sick. Monks copied manuscripts, and nuns did embroidery to decorate the churches.

Beliefs and miracles

Almost everyone believed that God was all-powerful and knew everything that happened in the world. They thought he would punish the bad and reward the good by sending them to Hell or Heaven when they died. They thought good harvests, droughts, illness, health, storms and wars all happened through the will of God. They asked for the help of priests to try and keep God happy and also visited the tombs of saints to ask for miracles.

Woods and Forests

In the Middle Ages, much of Europe was covered by forest. Most villages were at the edge of the forest, but some were deep in its heart. The forest provided food and wood for the peasants and a hunting ground for the nobility.

Information

■ A source of wood and charcoal

The forest provided the wood that people used to make everyday objects such as tools, plates, cups and furniture. They needed wood to build and repair their houses and barns, to make carts and boats, and to burn on their fires. Wood was also burned to make the charcoal used for smelting iron ore.

■ A source of free food

The peasants added variety to their diet by gathering nuts, fruits and berries from the forest. These included chestnuts and acorns, which were ground into flour. They also took their pigs to fatten up on fallen fruit and nuts. The forests were full of game, which belonged to the local lord – but the peasants often went poaching to catch partridges and hares.

■ A place of work and refuge

People who lived and worked in the forests included hermits and solitary monks, charcoal burners and iron-miners, and the lord's gamekeepers and warreners, who looked after his rabbit warrens. There were also runaway slaves, bandits and outlaws. The most famous was Robin Hood who lived in Sherwood Forest, but no one knows if he really existed.

■ A place of fear and enchantment

Many people were frightened of going into the forest alone, either by day or by night. As well as the obvious dangers of getting lost or attacked by wild animals, people thought there were fairies and witches. They also expected to meet legendary animals, such as unicorns and dragons.

Living in Towns

Towns grew in size and number during the Middle Ages, but only a few, such as London, York and Norwich, attracted very large populations.

Behind closed gates

Many medieval towns were surrounded by a high wall with gates to let people in or out. These gates were closed at night and in times of danger. Inside the gates, wooden houses were packed closely together around stone-built churches. Many houses had a workshop attached to them. In the garden, vegetables were grown and hens, geese and maybe a pig were kept for food.

Wealth and trade

Towns depended on trade for their existence. They all had a marketplace where peasants could sell their surplus crops and crafts people could sell cloth, furniture, tools, leather goods and metalware. There was also an annual fair to which merchants came from many parts of the country, often bringing luxury items such as silk and spices from overseas.

Fire, disease and famine

Fire was a constant danger in medieval towns because the wooden buildings and narrow streets allowed it to spread very quickly. People put their house-fires out at night, even in very cold weather. The unpaved streets had no drains, so germs bred rapidly in the waste and rubbish. The germs were spread by rats and caused disease. Famine was also a danger in times of war.

Information

Towns as independent states

Even the wealthiest towns in England had to obey the law of the king. In Europe, however, some rich towns in Flanders, northern France and Italy fought for their independence in the 10th century and became powerful states in their own right. Venice, in the north of Italy, was one of the richest states.

Cities in the Middle Ages

With 200,000 inhabitants each, Paris and Venice were the largest European cities in the 13th century. London was next, then Bruges and the German cities of Hanover and Lubeck.

Making

Anyone who was important had a seal. This was a piece of metal embossed with an emblem, which was imprinted into sealing wax. The seal was used to secure a confidential document, and was recognized as the signature of its owner.

You will need:
- a cork from a bottle
- a button with an embossed pattern
- some strong glue
- the wax coating from a cheese (such as a Babybel)

1. Put some glue on the cork.

2. Glue the button onto the cork. Leave it to dry.

a Seal

4. Push your seal into the centre of the wax.

3. Knead a ball of wax with your fingers. Then squash it with your thumb onto the document to be sealed.

Pilgrims and Travellers

Travelling was difficult and dangerous in the Middle Ages, so few people went far. Roads became impassable in wet weather, and there were few signposts and no maps. There was also a constant risk of attack by bandits and robbers.

◼ Methods of transport

The most common way of travelling was on foot, though the rich went on horseback. Journeys could take weeks, months or even years. It was often easier, but slower, to travel inland by boat along rivers and lakes.

◼ Pilgrimages abroad

The greatest medieval travellers were those who went abroad on pilgrimages. The most popular places were Rome, where the pope lived; Santiago de Compostella in Spain, where St James was buried; and Jerusalem, which was the site of Christ's tomb. At these places, the pilgrims touched the relics and asked to be cured of an illness or to have their sins forgiven.

Information

Pilgrimages in Britain

Those who could not go abroad on a pilgrimage paid someone else to go in their place, or they went to one of the holy shrines in Britain. The most popular shrine was that of Thomas à Becket in Canterbury. Others were St David's in Wales and Walsingham in Norfolk, where a vision of the Virgin Mary was seen in the 11th century.

Danger and hospitality

On the road pilgrims might meet up with fellow travellers, including merchants, soldiers, actors, minstrels and students. Or they might meet cut-throats who were prepared to kill to get some money. Pilgrims also had to be careful where they stayed overnight, as many isolated inns were hiding places for bandits. The safest places were monasteries or inns in towns.

The nobility travelled in covered wagons – but even these were not very comfortable, as the wooden wheels bumped along the unpaved roads.

Labourers an

There were many different industries, but textiles employed the most workers.

The windmill and the horizontal loom were both important inventions of the Middle Ages.

■ The expansion of industry

The development of the windmill and the water wheel at the beginning of the 12th century provided the power that made it possible for industry to expand in the Middle Ages. The power turned machinery to grind grain into flour, prepare animal skins for leather-making, and soften newly-woven cloth. In forges where tools and weapons were made, water wheels drove the bellows that made the fires hot enough to turn iron ore into metal.

■ Masters and labourers

Many people worked in small workshops attached to their homes. Some worked for themselves, but others worked for a master craftsman who paid them for the work they did. He would be a member of a guild, an organization that expected high standards of training and workmanship.

The best merchants sold silk and woollen cloth all over Europe. Many of them became very rich and powerful.

Master Craftsmen

■ Wool and cloth

At the start of the Middle Ages, England was a major exporter of raw wool, mainly to the textile cities of Bruges, Ypres and Douai in Flanders. By the 14th century, however, this had changed. The wool was spun and woven in England and exported to Europe as cloth.

■ A working family

Many peasants did not have enough land to support their families, so they needed to earn extra money as cloth-makers. The whole family was involved in the work. The children *carded* the raw wool, and the women spun it into yarn.

The men then wove the yarn into cloth on a loom and took it to market.

Carding is combing the tangles out of raw wool to make it straight and smooth before spinning it into yarn.

■ Luxury goods

Not all crafts people made everyday items. In large cities such as London and York they made clothes from silk and brocade, and from the fur of stoats and otters. Goldsmiths made plates, cups and jewellery decorated with precious stones. Cabinetmakers made beautifully-carved furniture. Their customers were the Church, the nobility and merchants.

Food and Drink

In the Middle Ages, food was often dull. But on feast days, meals for the rich became wonderful banquets of salmon, mutton, venison, even peacocks and swans.

Meat was roasted on a spit or stewed in a cauldron. Bread and pies baked in an oven at the side of the hearth.

The peasants' diet

The peasants' daily diet was coarse brown bread made from barley or rye, with cheese, vegetable soup or eggs. Occasionally they ate pork, chicken or duck, or game and fish they had poached.

The influence of the Church

The Church taught people that it was wrong to eat meat on a Friday and throughout the whole of Lent. Instead, they had to eat fish. The rich had their own fish-ponds, but the poor had to buy salted fish or poach it from the nearest river.

Meals for the rich

Except on Fridays, the rich had plenty of meat. They ate it from plates made of gold, silver or pewter, using a knife and their fingers, as forks had not been invented. It was difficult to feed animals over the winter, so many were killed in the autumn and the meat was salted to preserve it. This left a strong taste that was disguised by herbs and spices.

Ginger

Nutmeg

Cardamom

Cinnamon

Crusaders brought rare spices back from the Orient.

What did people drink?

Water came from streams and rivers where people washed themselves and their clothes and where animals stood to drink. In towns, the tanneries and dye-works also polluted the water. So the rich drank wine and the poor drank beer or cider. Although it was made from water, the alcohol helped to kill the germs.

Prepare a Medieval Meal

In the Middle Ages, a slice of stale bread called a trencher was used as a plate.

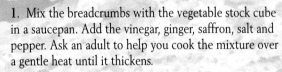

 Green egg and cheese broth (for 4 people)

You will need:
- 3 slices of toast made into crumbs (or 100 g of breadcrumbs)
- 1 vegetable stock cube
- 1 dessertspoon of vinegar
- 1 pinch of powdered ginger
- 1 pinch of saffron
- salt and pepper
- 8 eggs
- 1 dessertspoon of chopped parsley
- 70 g of grated cheese

1. Mix the breadcrumbs with the vegetable stock cube in a saucepan. Add the vinegar, ginger, saffron, salt and pepper. Ask an adult to help you cook the mixture over a gentle heat until it thickens.

2. Ask the adult to bring a saucepan of water to the boil. Poach the eggs by breaking them gently one at a time into the boiling water. Cook for two minutes.

3. Lift the eggs out of the saucepan with a fish slice. Put them on the trenchers without breaking them.

4. Add the chopped parsley and grated cheese to the breadcrumb mixture and pour it over the eggs.

An Activity

Fruit turnover
(especially for Lent)

You will need:
- 3 apples
- 100 g of figs
- 70 g of shelled nuts
- 100 g of raisins
- 2 dessertspoons of honey
- 1 teaspoon of cinnamon
- 1 teaspoon of ground ginger
- 200 g of ready-made pastry

1. Ask an adult to help you put the raisins into boiling water so that they swell up.

2. Chop the apples, figs and nuts into small pieces. Dry the raisins and mix everything together.

3. Add the honey and spices.

4. Cut out circles of pastry and spoon some of the fruit mixture into the middle of each of them.

5. Wet the edges of the pastry and shape it into turnovers. Seal the edges by pressing with the teeth of a fork.

6. Ask an adult to put the turnovers in the oven at 180°C (Gas Mark 6) for 30 minutes.

Almond milk
(for 4 people)

You will need:
- 1 slice of stale bread, toasted
- 100 g of ground almonds
- 1 dessertspoon of orange flower water
- 250 ml of milk
- 2 dessertspoons of honey

Put the ingredients into a saucepan and ask an adult to boil the mixture for five minutes. Blend in a food processor, then filter through a fine sieve. Delicious!

Diseases and Medicine

When the plague struck, so many people died that there was not enough time to dig individual graves. Large numbers were buried together each day.

Poor living conditions and very few doctors meant that many people died young.

Surviving childhood

Many children died within a few days of being born. Those who survived were then at risk from diseases such as whooping cough and measles. These were often fatal, partly because no one knew how to treat them properly, partly because many children were weakened by malnutrition.

■ Fevers and epidemics

In the Middle Ages, no one really understood how diseases spread or the importance of being clean. The water people drank was often contaminated, while the food they ate was usually no longer fresh. Their clothes were often damp as well as dirty, and there were rats and mice in their houses. Fevers and epidemics, such as influenza and smallpox, killed thousands every year.

■ The Black Death

The worst epidemic of all was the Black Death, a plague which swept across Europe from Asia in the 14th century. Spread by rats and fleas on traders' ships, it reached Genoa in Italy in 1347. A year later, it reached southern England and quickly spread north. The plague affected rich and poor alike and probably killed about half the population of England.

Dead bodies were collected in horse-drawn carts.

■ Healers and bonesetters

In most villages there was someone who knew how to set broken bones and how to make ointments and medicines from herbs, minerals and parts of birds and animals. Some also made charms to try and stop people getting ill in the first place. In towns, barbers did simple surgery. Trained doctors were rare and expensive and often no more successful

Outsiders

Strangers, beggars, lepers and people with different beliefs were all treated with suspicion and even hostility.

Beggars

In the Middle Ages, many people fell on hard time. If illness or injury made it impossible for them to work, they usually had to take up begging in order to survive. Many beggars lived quietly, but some formed into gangs to go robbing and murdering.

The Knights of St John cared for the sick, then fought in the crusades.

Lepers

Lepers had a contagious disease called leprosy, which affected their skin and eyes and eventually caused their fingers and toes to drop off. There was no cure, so other people were terrified of catching it. Because of this, they made lepers live outside the towns and only allowed them in if they rang a handbell to warn everyone of their approach.

Jewish communities

Small numbers of Jews lived in many of the larger towns of medieval England, such as York and Lincoln. Many were successful businessmen and some even lent money to the king. Other people were wary of them because they followed a different religion. They were often persecuted and attacked when things went wrong.

■ Crusades against the Muslims

By the Middle Ages, Muslims had control of Spain and southern Italy. They also controlled *Jerusalem*, a place of pilgrimage for Christians. They got on well with the Christians until 1095, when the pope decided that Muslims were allied to the Devil and sent an army of knights on the First Crusade to take Jerusalem out of their control. The crusades went on into the 13th century but eventually failed.

Jerusalem was a sacred city to the Muslims, Jews and Christians. It is still fought over today.

Incredibl

KINGS WHO PERFORMED MIRACLES

Medieval people thought that kings represented God on Earth. They also thought they could perform miracles. In France, after a king had been crowned at Reims, people suffering from scrofula – a disease caused by malnutrition and sometimes called the King's Evil – came to him for help. He touched them and a doctor then declared that all traces of the disease had vanished. "The king touched you, the king healed you," he told them.

ANIMALS OF WAR

During the Hundred Years' War (1337–1453) the English archers had deadly accurate bows made from yew wood with strings made from pigs' guts. Before the Battle of Agincourt (October 25, 1415) the French sent rats into the English camp, hoping they would eat the bow strings. The English were prepared for this, however, and had brought cats with them to guard their bows. Each army also took ferocious dogs to war, but cut off their ears and tails so that the enemy could not catch them.

but True!

PRECIOUS RELICS

Almost every church and monastery wanted to attract pilgrims because of the money they brought with them. There were not enough true relics to go round, so many were fakes, but people wanted to believe that the items they saw really were genuine. People went to Saint Riquier in northern France to see a piece of Christ's robe, a morsel of bread he had given to his disciples, some milk from the Virgin Mary, some hairs from St Paul's beard and the stones which had been used to kill St Stephen and were still covered in his blood.

CONVERTING UNBELIEVERS

The Holy Roman Emperor Charlemagne (742–814) forced unbelievers to convert to Christianity by burning down their villages. Two centuries earlier, St Columban had used a more peaceful method to convert the Irish who had massacred missionaries. When he arrived in a village, he knelt down, crossed his arms and stayed as still as a statue for hours, days or sometimes even weeks. The people were so intrigued and impressed that they ended up by joining him. By the year 1000, almost the whole of Europe was converted to Christianity.

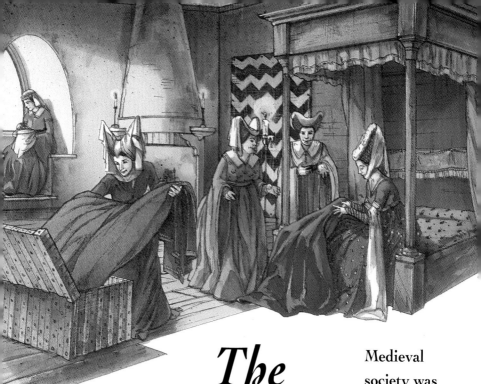

The Role of Women

Medieval society was dominated by men, but women played an essential role in the home, the workplace and the farm.

■ Working women

Apart from the very rich, wives looked after the house and the children, cooked meals, brewed beer and made clothes. In the country they also collected firewood, looked after the animals and worked in the fields. In town,s they might help their husbands in business. Even when they were pregnant they kept working, only stopping long enough to give birth.

■ The lady's chamber

In the castles and manor houses of the rich, the women had their own separate world. The lord's wife organized the servants who cooked and cleaned, kept the fires burning and helped to look after the children. The lady had her own chamber where she sat with her companions, passing the time with embroidery, gossip and singing.

■ Courtly love

At first knights were often brutal towards women, but slowly their attitude changed. By the 13th century, they treated women of their own class with chivalry and good manners. Nearly every knight had a lady whom he loved passionately – though she might be someone else's wife. He wore her colours in battles and in tournaments and was willing to die for her.

Isabella of Castile

■ Heroines and witches

In the 12th century, the most venerated woman was the Virgin Mary, mother of Jesus, and many churches were dedicated to her in this period. Other important medieval women were queens such as Isabella of Castile, who with her husband reunited Spain, and wealthy abbesses such as St Hilda of Whitby. In France, the warrior Joan of Arc was a heroine, but the English burned her as a witch in 1431.

Joan of Arc was a peasant girl who had a vision telling her to lead the French army against the English at Orleans in the Hundred Years' War.

Hygiene and Beauty

Most homes in the Middle Ages did not have bathrooms or indoor lavatories. There was no running water and all clothes had to be washed by hand.

▪ Taking a bath

Most people thought they were clean enough if they occasionally washed their hands and face with water. Some of the rich did take a bath, but not very often. They sat in a large wooden tub which had to be filled with water from the well or the river, and cleaned themselves with soap made from a mixture of animal fat and wood ash.

▪The war against lice

In medieval times, there were no insecticides, so people were constanly irritated by fleas and lice. Despite the itching, well-mannered people tried not to scratch in public, but they felt free to do so when they were at home. As they chatted, they looked out for fleas and lice on their clothes.

Information

▓ Very basic hygiene!

With no toothbrushes or toothpaste, people
cleaned their teeth by rubbing them with salt or
soot. They washed their clothes occasionally in the
river or a tub, stamping on them to remove the
dirt. In the 13th century, lavatories were built
inside castles and the waste from them went into
the moat. Everyone else used an outside lavatory,
which stank atrociously and attracted all the flies.

▓ Filthy streets and filthy houses

Most streets in towns and villages were unpaved.
Animals wandered along them and went into
the houses. People threw all sorts of waste out
of their windows, which added to the
rubbish in the road. The houses
themselves were often infested
with rats, mice, frogs, beetles,
cockroaches, fleas, flies and
bugs of all
descriptions.

▓ The cover-up

The rich
rubbed
perfumed oils and
ointments into their skin and avoided
bad breath by chewing cinnamon,
liquorice and fennel. Women washed
their hair in herb-scented shampoos
and hid bad complexions with white

Clothes and Fashion

Above all else, clothes had to be practical and warm because houses were poorly heated and people also spent a lot of time out of doors.

■ Everyday clothes

The different classes of people in medieval society could easily be recognized by their everyday clothing and the material it was made from. Peasants and labourers usually wore ill-fitting trousers, shirts and coats made from rough woollen cloth. Their wives wore long kirtles or gowns of the same material. In contrast, wealthy men and women wore well-fitted clothes of fine wool, linen, silk and brocade, a heavy fabric with a raised design.

Elaborate hats and headdresses were popular with the wealthy throughout the Middle Ages and were even worn indoors.

■ Pointed hats and pointed shoes

Towards the end of the Middle Ages, wealthy women styled their hair in the shape of a cone, over which they wore a tall pointed hat known as a hennin or steeple-hat. The men drew attention to their feet by wearing very long shoes with pointed toes.

■ Fur, fur and more fur

By the 14th century, the climate had turned much colder in Europe. Wolves roamed in the forests and their skins were much sought after to line coats and capes for the rich. Rabbit and fox fur were also used, as were otter and sable, and soft white ermine was used for hems. Squirrel skin was made into warm slippers.

■ Fashionable shades

The clothes of the poor were usually dull brown or grey, but the rich could afford expensively-dyed cloth. Colours went in and out of fashion, but included red, green, purple, blue, bright brown and yellow. Priests and monks wore black, brown or white, which symbolized purity. But no one wore striped clothes, for fear of attracting the Devil.

Festivals and Carnivals

Religious festivals ofteninculded many games and a great deal of merrymaking.

■ Holy days and holidays

On holy days, religious festivals were held in villages and towns, and no work was done. The main holy days were Christmas and Easter, celebrating the birth and death of Jesus. Also important were the Feast of the Virgin Mary on August 15th and the Feast of Corpus Christi on June 8th.

▨ Street entertainment

On the most important holy days, people would gather in the streets to watch actors perform in a mystery play. This told the life of a saint, or a story from the Bible. It was usually acted on a cart, which was pulled from street to street. While they waited, the crowds were often entertained by jugglers, acrobats, fire-eaters, jesters and musicians.

▨ Maypoles and bonfires

Not all festivals in England tied in with Christianity. Although remnants of pre-Christian pagan times had been banned, dancing round maypoles, lighting bonfires and a belief in the spirit world still continued in country areas.

▨ Hullabaloos

Young people also organized festivities that had nothing to do with religion. Hullabaloos celebrated anything that was a little bit different. For example, if an old man married a young woman, or vice versa, people would stand in front of their house in the middle of the night, shouting loudly and banging saucepans together.

A feast in the castle

This scene takes place at the height of the Middle Ages, around AD 1100. The artist's brush has made a number of mistakes – 19 in all. Can you find them?

Solution on p. 63

Churche

The greatest work of the Middle Ages was the building of churches.

■ Huge building sites

It was very expensive to build a church and the work could last for decades or even a century. Each project had a team of specialists, including masons, carpenters, glaziers and sculptors, led by an architect.

The cathedral of Notre-Dame in Paris was started in 1163 and most of it was finished by 1245.

■ Romanesque buildings

At first, medieval builders copied Roman techniques for their churches. Built from stone or brick, their churches had rounded vaults, partly supported by cylindrical pillars. Thick walls carried most of the weight. There were no mechanical diggers or cranes – all the work was done by hand, with scaffolding, pulleys and great skill.

The Romanesque church of Sainte-Foy de Conques

ɪnd Cathedrals

The Gothic cathedral of Notre-Dame in Paris

◼ Gothic architecture

At the end of the 11th century, a new technique that became known as Gothic architecture was used. The weight of the building was supported on the pillars, rather than the walls. This meant that the walls could have large ornate windows and the vault could be over 35 m high. This style developed in the area around Paris, and from it there spread throughout Europe.

◼ Images in stone, glass and wood

Both Romanesque and Gothic churches had carvings and statues in stone and wood, as well as stained glass windows. Most showed scenes from the Bible or represented Jesus, his family or his disciples and other saints. In England, some carvings also showed comical scenes from everyday life.

◼ Church schools

All cathedrals and some churches had small schools where young men learned to become priests. As towns expanded, however, many wealthy families wanted their children to learn to read and count so that they could run successful businesses – and so they too started going to the church schools. From the 13th century the first universities appeared in Oxford, Paris and Bologna (in Italy). They trained men to be priests, lawyers and

Gargoyles on Gothic churches were often carved to look like dragons or grimacing demons.

Feudal Society

During the Middle Ages, many countries in Europe were ruled by strong and powerful kings. Only the pope in Rome had more power.

■ The role of the king

In medieval times, the king was thought to be God's representative on Earth. He governed alone and his word was law. He also led his army into battle. However, if he died without heirs, or if his successor was still a child, rebellious relations or nobles might try to take the throne and start a new dynasty.

The sceptre was the symbol of the king's supreme power and the crown a symbol of his dignity.

Information

Feudal society was made up of nobles, clergymen and workers.

■ The social hierarchy

Feudal society was divided into three main groups. Most important were the nobles and the clergymen, who between them held most of the land. Beneath them came everyone else – bankers, merchants, crafts people, and then the peasants. They did most of the work but had no control over what happened to them.

■ The nobility

The nobility held vast amounts of land from the king. In exchange, they fought on his behalf. To help them in this, they had many retainers, or vassals. These were the knights who raised armies for the king. Some lived at the castle, others were given land that was divided into manors with peasants to do the work.

■ The clergy

Bishops and abbots were in charge of the Church. They had a great deal of influence and usually came from wealthy families. In contrast, the parish priests were often poor and sometimes not even well-educated.

■ Merchants and bankers

Rich people who made their wealth as merchants or bankers played an important role in the towns they lived in, but they usually had no real power.

The Art of Warfare

The noblemen who held the land in medieval times were also the chief warriors, often leading their men into battle for the king.

Knights

The most fearsome warriors were knights on horseback. They wore a coat of mail and armour made of plates of steel, and covered their head with a helmet. They were armed with a lance and a sword, which they used in the service of God and King. A horse and armour cost a lot of money, so only the rich could afford to equip themselves for battle.

A suit of armour could weigh as much as 25 kg.

A joust

Information

Training to be a knight

A nobleman started training to be a knight when he was very young. Known as a page, he learned manners, swordplay and horse-riding. At 13 he went to war with his lord as a squire, and at 16 he was ready to become a knight. After a night of prayer, he knelt before his lord, who dubbed him a knight either by tapping him on the nape of his neck, or on the shoulder with a sword.

A page learned the art of warfare alongside a king or a nobleman.

Jousts and tournaments

A knight spent long hours on his horse chasing wild game. This accustomed him to the fatigue and pain he would face in battle. So did challenging another knight to a jousting match at a tournament. When they were jousting, the knights never struck to kill, but only to show how skilled and brave they were.

Foot-soldiers

In battle the knights were assisted by foot-soldiers, who were armed with pikes and daggers. At first these were men from the knight's estate, who fought with him in part payment for the land they farmed. Later they were professional soldiers, paid money and trained properly.

The squire helped the knight get ready for battle.

Battle tactics

Large battles were very rare. In the Hundred Years' War, 10,000 to 15,000 Englishmen fought against a similar number of French. A battle started with a cavalry charge, followed by hand-to-hand fighting. By the end of the 14th century, simple cannons and other guns were used, but for many years they were more noisy than accurate.

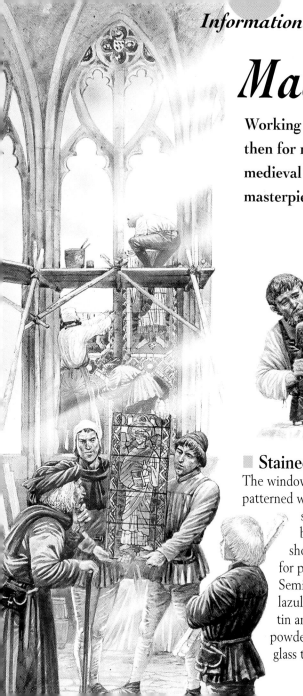

Masterpiece

Working first for the Church, then for royalty and nobility, medieval artists produced many masterpieces.

■ Stained glass windows

The windows in Gothic churches were patterned with stained glass in rich shades of blue, red, green, brown and yellow. They showed scenes from the Bible for people who could not read. Semi-precious stones such as lapis lazuli, and minerals such as iron, tin and copper were crushed into powder and added to the molten glass to give the rich colours.

f the Middle Ages

Illuminated manuscripts

The first printed books in Europe were produced by Johann Gutenberg in 1455. Before that, books were copied by hand, usually by monks. Some manuscripts were plain, others had illuminated (decorated) capital letters, and whole pages of flowers, animals and Biblical scenes in coloured inks and gold leaf.

Landscapes and portraits

Most paintings had a religious theme. At first they were mainly portraits of Jesus, his family, or some of the saints. All the characters looked majestic, but they also looked stiff and unnatural. From the 13th century onwards, painters in Italy and Flanders started to paint a landscape into the background of their pictures. Then nobles and rich merchants began to have their own portraits painted to look like the saints they wanted to protect them.

Angelic music

Music was written mostly for the Church, rather than as entertainment. Monks tried to imitate the choir of angels that they believed surrounded God. Their songs were unaccompanied (performed without instruments), and everyone sang the same tune at the same time. This was known as 'plain chant'. From the 11th century, music was written on scales of notes, with melodies for several voices.

The horse-collar allowed a ploughing team to pull loads that were six times heavier than before.

False. The team could pull loads that were twice as heavy as before.

The largest European city in the Middle Ages was Rome.

False. The two largest were Paris and Venice, followed by London.

Fallow was the name for a tax on bread.

False. Fallow meant ground that was left uncultivated for a year.

Large fairs attracted merchants and traders from many parts of Europe.

True. Fairs were good places to do business.

There were often fields and meadows within medieval towns.

True. Some townspeople kept cows that could graze there.

Women did not work in the Middle Ages.

False. They worked in the home and on the farms. Many also worked as servants in castles and manor houses.

When a young noble became a knight, his lord gave him a sharp blow of the hand on the nape of his neck.

True. This ceremony was called dubbing.

Gothic architecture started in Ile-de-France in Paris.

True. The earliest surviving Gothic building is the abbey of Saint-Denis in Paris, which was started around 1140.

Before the 13th century, windows were closed with wooden shutters.

True. Medieval people knew how to make glass, but it was too expensive to use for houses.

A knight's armour often weighed 25 kg.

True. It was made from plates of steel or iron riveted onto leather.

Kings were elected by an assembly of the people.

False. Many of them fought their way to their position. Each one then tried to hand the title of king down to his eldest son.

Cheques date back to the Middle Ages.

True. They were used by merchants who did not want to carry a lot of money with them.

■ **Medieval people had to pay a tax to cross bridges and enter towns.**

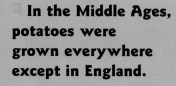 ■ **In the Middle Ages, potatoes were grown everywhere except in England.**

False. The potato, which originated in South America, was unknown in medieval Europe. Explorers introduced them to Europe in the 16th century.

■ **In trials, many suspects were tortured to make them confess.**

True. Among other things, they could be stretched on the rack, crushed under increasingly heavy weights, whipped, branded, or have their eyes poked out.

Anyone who was suspected of being a witch could be burnt alive.

True. They could also be drowned or hanged.

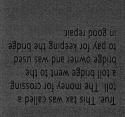

True. This tax was called a toll. The money for crossing a toll bridge went to the bridge owner and was used to pay for keeping the bridge in good repair.

Index

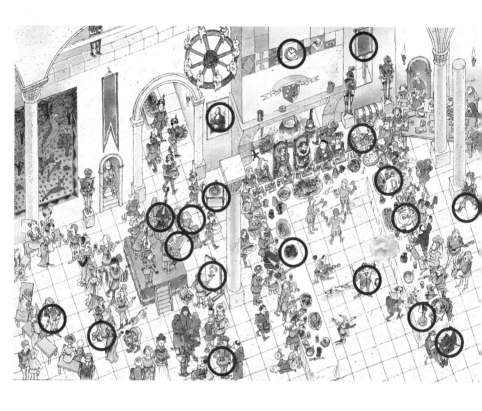

Solution to the game on pages 48-49

You should have found a clock (a 17th century invention), the Mona Lisa (painted by
Leonardo da Vinci in 1503), a roller blind (20th century), a bass player (modern), a printed
book (1447), a pencil (invented in 1795), a trolley with castors (19th century), a fork with
four prongs (16th century), a pitcher with a cork (16th century), china plates (in the
Middle Ages, a wealthy host might have had pewter plates), a saltcellar (salt at this time
was put on the table in a little wooden bowl), tomatoes (the tomato did not appear in
Europe until 1596 and was not eaten until much later as people suspected it contained a
powerful poison), a stethoscope (19th century), a fob watch (1675), striped clothes
(medieval people believed that striped clothes would call up the Devil), a zip (1851),
stiletto heels, boots and a tie.

Created by Marie-Odile Fordacq
Authors évelyne Brisou-Pellen, Béatrice Garel, Catherine Pauwels, Antoine Sabbagh
Managing editors Marie-Odile Fordacq, Camilla Hallinan
Editorial co-ordinators Ariane Léandri, Molly Perham
Art editors Sue Aldworth, Ch'en Ling, Bernard Girodroux, Val Pidgeon
Illustrators Ian Chamberlain, Peter Dennis, Francesca D'Ottavi, Jeff Fisher,
Daniel Guerrier, Nick Hall, Clare Melinsky, Nicki Palin, Richard Ward
Activities Ting Morris, Tim Ridley Photography, Val Wright
Photo research Veneta Bullen

Photo credits AKG London, Bibliothèque Nationale Paris, Bridgeman Art Library (Bibliothèque Royal de Belgique,
Brussels; Bibliothèque Nationale Paris; British Library; Giraudon; Musee Conde, Chantilly; Kuntshistorisches Museum
Vienna); CADW Photographic Library Cardiff, et archives, Michael Holford, Angelo Hornak Library, Robert Harding,
Koninklijk Museum voor Schone Kunsten Antwerpen, Metropolitan Museum of Art New York, Public Records Office,
Royal Library Copenhagen, Scala, Sothebys UK, Wellcome Institute Library London
Design and page make-up équipage, Olivier Lemoine, Judy Linard, Terry Woodley

KINGFISHER
An imprint of Kingfisher Publications Plc
New Penderel House, 283–288 High Holborn, London WC1V 7HZ

This edition first published by Kingfisher Publications Plc 1998
Originally published in France by Nathan
under the title *Megascope: La vie au Moyen âge*

2 4 6 8 10 9 7 5 3 1

A CIP catalogue record for this book is available
from the British Library

ISBN 07534 0 224 6

Printed in Italy

Stickers

Italian armour, 15th century

Wooden chest, 15th century

Coat of arms of René d'Anjou, 15th century

Dancing

Jug in the shape of a griffin, end of the 12th century

Knight on a caparisoned horse (richly dressed for a joust)

Trade sign

Stickers

A scribe writing on parchment, from an illuminated manuscript

Reliquary (container for relics), 1220

Musician and juggler

The angel of death

Crossbow

Chess players, 14th century

Clothes worn by doctors during the plague. The beak was filled with sweet-smelling herbs.